"STILL FUNCTIONING, DREAMING, BUILDING, HEALING, AND MAINTAINING"

" THE BLACK WOMAN IS GOD"

"STILL FUNCTIONING, DREAMING, BUILDING, HEALING, AND MAINTAINING"

"The Black Woman is God"

MARIE BREVIL

MY LITTL' WORKSHOP

For permission requests, contact:
Marie Brevil or My Littl' Workshop

This book is a work of truth, spirit, and lived experience. While it may reference spiritual practices, ancestral wisdom, and energetic principles, it is not intended to replace medical, psychological, or professional advice. The author shares this work with deep respect for all cultures, lineages, and spiritual expressions.

Printed in the United States of America
First Edition – 2025
Cover Design & Interior Layout by:
Marie Brevil & Prince Jai
Published by: My Littl'Workshop
Dedicated to all Indigenous Women reclaiming their crowns. Your voice. Your essence. Your legacy. May this work honor it all.

Preface: Reclaiming Identity, Refocusing Energy

If you've been following me for a while, you know I usually steer clear of the political noise. The endless back-and-forth, the conflicting narratives—it drains the energy we need for what truly matters: our growth, our healing, and our power.

In many circles, the words Black and Blackness are loaded with so many meanings—too many of them harmful, diminishing, and designed to obscure our truth. But today, let's reclaim and upgrade the language we use. Let's think of ourselves as Indigenous: the first, the original, the main, the unlimited. These are the titles that carry the weight of our power and the brightness of our legacy.

Yes, in politics and other spaces, these words are twisted —Black is sometimes coded as dead, childlike, or minor, derogatory titles meant to reduce and disempower. But we don't have to accept those meanings. It's all in the mind, all in the intention behind the words we choose.
We call our men Kings—royalty in every sense. And our women? We call them Queans—with an "A"—because that is the original, sacred name for the woman who leads, nurtures, and reigns. Not "queen," which historically has meant concubine or prostitute. Our language must honor our true selves and our sacred roles.

So, let's take this trip together. Let's rise above distractions and noise. Let's not get tangled with those who are only now encountering truths they should have mastered long ago. Stay focused on you, because you are worth it.

Focus on your growth, your healing, your purpose— then worry about the rest later.

How to Use This Book

This is not just a book. It is a mirror. A journal. A scripture. A companion. A tool for spiritual, emotional, ancestral, and mental realignment.

You do not need to rush. You are not behind. You are exactly where you are supposed to be, and this book meets you there.

❯ Breathe First

Before each session with this book, take a deep breath. Light a candle if you'd like. Create a sacred space—even if just within your spirit. Approach each page with presence, not pressure.

❯ Read with Intuition

You may read this book in order from front to back—or you may open it to the chapter your spirit leads you to in the moment. Trust your intuition. It always knows what you need.

❯ Journal and Reflect

Use the affirmations, declarations, and invocations as prompts for journaling. Reflect. Write in the margins. Speak the prayers aloud. Make this book yours. Let it evolve with you.

❯ Speak It, Don't Just Read It

This book is alive. Let your voice activate its power. Speak the affirmations out loud. Whisper the declarations into your day. Repeat the invocations as often as needed. Let the vibration move through your being.

❯ Use It as Spiritual Maintenance

Return to this book when you need reminding. When you're tired of being strong. When you're ready to rebuild. When you feel like you're losing yourself again. This is your tool for maintenance, not just for breakthrough moments.

❯ Share as You're Led

If a chapter speaks to you deeply, share it with your sisters, your daughters, your tribe. But only share from overflow. Protect your energy and sacred revelations first.

This book is for you, but also through you.
For the generations before, the generations after, and most importantly—for you now.

Use it with intention. Use it with reverence. Use it with truth.
Because you are worth the restoration.
You are worthy of your own becoming.
You are divine.

Introduction

To every woman who has ever had to function through her pain, dream while bleeding, build with broken bricks, and heal silently—we see you. This book is your mirror, your altar, your reminder. It is not here to tell you who you are, but to awaken what has always been true within you.

You are not just surviving—you are divine. You are the blueprint, the builder, the healer, the oracle. You are the force that keeps the world spinning while often being overlooked. But no more.

This is a sacred offering to remind you: You are the God you've been waiting for.

It's time to rise, rebuild, and reclaim—without apology. This is your time.

And so it is.

Light over Darkness

Chapter 1: Moving While Mourning, Healing While Hurting

She rises before the sun, not always because she wants to, but because she must. There are people who depend on her. Children, partners, coworkers, elders. There is a world that she must show up for—even when that same world refuses to show up for her. She pours from wells that were never refilled, gives from a heart that often goes unheld, and offers wisdom that others appropriate while leaving her unseen. Yet she continues. She functions.

What many don't understand is that functioning is not the same as being whole. The indigenous woman, the Black woman, has been conditioned to equate survival with strength, to see suffering as a badge of honor. They call her resilient when what they really mean is overburdened. They admire her perseverance, but they never question why she has to endure so much in the first place. She's expected to show up with a smile even when she's spiritually hemorrhaging.

Behind her eyes are galaxies of grief. Grief for the dreams she delayed. Grief for the ancestors who were never mourned properly. Grief for the younger self that had to grow up too soon. Still, she goes on—drying her own tears in the silence of the night and waking before dawn to do it all over again.

Her pain is ancient, passed down like a sacred story rewritten in every lifetime. But what they forget is that her resilience is ancient too. It is carved in her bones, encrypted in her blood. She is functioning not just out of habit, but out of a sacred memory of what it means to carry nations inside a single body. Her healing is silent but sacred. Even when she's hurting, she nurtures others. Even when she's drowning, she teaches others how to swim.

But today, we speak to her. The Divine One. The God-body walking through a world that cannot comprehend her frequency. We acknowledge that functioning is not freedom. That survival is not enough. That pretending to be okay is no longer acceptable.

This is a space for her to pause. To exhale. To unmask. To be held. To be reminded that even when she is tired, she is still sacred. Even when she is grieving, she is still God.

PRAYER: For the Woman Who Functions While in Pain

Divine Mother who moves through me,
I call to you not in performance, but in honesty.
I am tired. I am heavy. I am still showing up,
but I need space to fall apart.
Wrap me in the arms of ancestors who see me.
Let me rest in your eternal lap, just for a moment.
Heal the places I don't speak of.
Knit together the torn edges of my soul.
Remind me that I am worthy of peace,
not just perseverance.
I am your daughter. Your reflection. Your resurrection.
Let your grace move through my weariness,
and let me remember:
I do not have to carry everything alone.

INVOCATION: To the Circle of Divine Mothers

I call on the mothers before me—
Those who labored in silence
Those who healed others while dying inside
Those who laughed with cracked ribs and broken hearts
Come, sit with me. Sing to my bones.
Bring your fire into my spirit and
your waters into my wounds.
Let the medicine in my blood remember its purpose.
Let the memory of my wholeness return to me.

I summon the power of the feminine divine
To awaken the part of me that still believes
I deserve ease.

AFFIRMATIONS: Speak These Over Your Spirit

- I am allowed to be tired and still be divine.
- My softness does not make me weak. My vulnerability is sacred.
- I release the lie that I have to be everything to everyone.
- I deserve spaces where I can fall apart and be rebuilt.
- Even when I'm hurting, I am still holy.
- I am a living altar—worthy of rest, worthy of love, worthy of light.

DECLARATIONS: Claim These as Your Truth

- I declare that I am no longer available for emotional labor that empties me.
- I declare that I will prioritize my peace as much as I've prioritized everyone else's.
- I declare that I will not minimize my pain just to maintain appearances.
- I declare that I am sacred, even in my mess, even in my mourning.
- I declare that from this day forward, I will treat myself like the temple I am.

Chapter 2: The Silent Superwoman Syndrome

They call her Superwoman, but it's not always a compliment. Sometimes, it's a silent curse disguised as praise. They admire how she holds everything together without falling apart—but they never ask what it costs her. They expect her to be the first to show up and the last to leave, to carry everyone's burdens on her back, even when her own heart is collapsing under the weight.

This is the Silent Superwoman Syndrome: where she's expected to do it all, fix it all, be it all, without ever asking for help. Her strength is demanded but rarely reciprocated. Her care is consumed but rarely replenished. She becomes the counselor, the nurse, the teacher, the prayer warrior, the parent, the provider, and the protector—all rolled into one—while no one checks in to see if she's okay.

She smiles when she's breaking. She works when she's sick. She leads while she's bleeding—sometimes literally. She comforts others while she cries behind closed doors. She teaches others how to love themselves while struggling to find reasons to love herself. And still, they applaud her strength.

But strength is not the absence of pain. It is not the refusal to rest. It is not the erasure of your own needs to fulfill someone else's expectations. True strength is knowing when to stop. When to say no.

When to choose yourself. When to break the cycle that says you must always perform to be worthy of love or respect.

There is nothing divine about self-abandonment. The Indigenous woman is not here to be the world's mule or its martyr. She is not here to save everyone at the expense of herself. Her existence is sacred even when she's not performing. Her worth is eternal, even when she's still. She doesn't need to explain her boundaries. She doesn't need to justify her rest. She is not a machine. She is a miracle.

The Silent Superwoman is being laid to rest. Not because she failed—but because she's finally choosing to live.

PRAYER: For the One Who's Tired of Being Everything

Mother of Mercy,
I come to you bare—no mask, no cape, no applause.
I lay down the armor I never asked for.
I release the roles I was never meant to hold alone.
Heal the spaces where I've confused survival for strength.
Wrap me in the truth that I am enough, even when I do nothing.
Let me rest without guilt. Let me pause without fear.
Let me return to myself, not as a role, but as a soul.

15

INVOCATION: To the Sacred Feminine Within

I call upon the One who knows herself beyond labor.
The One who is holy not because of what she does—but because of who she is.
Come forward, sit with me in this stillness.
Let the sacred silence speak where noise once covered the ache.
Return my spirit to its rhythm.
Return my soul to its sovereignty.
I am not your worker—I am your daughter.
I reclaim my right to just be.

AFFIRMATIONS: Repeat Until You Remember

- I am not responsible for everyone's healing.
- I am allowed to rest without explanation.
- My softness is powerful. My stillness is productive.
- I no longer betray myself to be liked, loved, or needed.
- I am not their superhero—I am my own sanctuary.

DECLARATIONS: Say It, Mean It, Live It
- I declare the end of over-functioning in spaces that deplete me.
- I declare peace over my nervous system and joy in my breath.
- I declare that I will no longer prove my worth through suffering.

- I declare that my body, my time, and my energy are sacred.
- I declare that from this moment on, I move like I know I am divine.

Chapter 3: The Power in Her Vision

They may try to distract her, delay her, detour her—but they cannot kill her vision. Because it was never hers alone. It was ancestral. It was divine. It was encoded into her spirit before she even took form in her mother's womb. The vision she carries is sacred—it is the continuation of her bloodline's prayers, prophecies, and promises. It is not a dream born of fantasy, but of memory.

The Indigenous woman—whom they label Black, but who is rooted deeper than color—sees beyond what the eyes can hold. Her vision is cosmic. Her intuition, surgical. She sees patterns before they unfold. She dreams futures while others are still clinging to the past. And this frightens people. Because what she sees, she builds. What she imagines, she births. And what she touches, she blesses.

They've tried to convince her she's crazy. That she's unstable. That her dreams are too big, too loud, too much. They've tried to reduce her visions to coincidences, and her instincts to emotions. But she remembers. Even when the world tries to erase her wisdom, she remembers.

Her vision is not meant to be palatable. It's meant to shift timelines. It's meant to birth revolutions. She is the mother of innovation, the oracle of divine design.

The worlds they inhabit were first seen in her sleep. She is not delusional—she is prophetic. And now, she must protect that vision like it is her last breath.

No more sharing dreams with people who only come to copy. No more building for communities that only extract. No more offering her blueprint to those who only want the benefit, not the source. Her vision is sacred, and it must be guarded accordingly.

This chapter is a call to every Indigenous woman to return to her inner vision. To clear the fog that others have placed in front of her third eye. To remember what she saw before the trauma, before the distractions, before the conditioning. To realign with her soul's design. This time, she doesn't just dream it. She protects it. She builds it. And she lives it.

PRAYER: For the Woman With Vision Too Big to Cage

Divine Mother,
Open my eyes beyond the surface.
Remove the veils, remove the illusions.
Restore to me the visions I forgot,

the dreams I abandoned,
And the purpose I almost gave away.
Let me trust what I see in the unseen.
Let me remember that the vision in me
was planted by You.
Help me protect it, grow it,
and walk in it unapologetically.
Let no delay, no enemy, no fear stop
what was already written.

INVOCATION: To the Seer Within

I call upon the Prophetess within me.
The one who sees without needing proof.
The one who dreams not for herself alone, but for generations.
Rise now. Clear the path.
Let your eyes speak truth into this moment.
Let your clarity burn away confusion.
Let your divine sight order my steps.
I remember now.
I am the vision.
I am the vessel.
I am the voice.

AFFIRMATIONS: Reclaim Your Sight

- My vision is divine, and I will no longer dim it.
- I am allowed to dream bigger than the box they put me in.

- I am building what my ancestors only whispered about.
- My intuition is my compass, and I trust where it leads me.
- I do not need validation when I have vision.

DECLARATIONS: Stand In It Boldly

- I declare that no one else will steward my dreams for me.
- I declare that my visions will manifest into reality with divine timing.
- I declare that I am protected from spiritual plagiarism and destiny theft.
- I declare that my clarity grows daily, and my purpose is unfolding now.
- I declare that I am the dream and the dreamer, the prophecy and the fulfillment.

Chapter 4: They Try to Distract Her From Her Destiny

They don't need to kill her to destroy her—just distract her. The world has mastered the art of interruption when it comes to the Indigenous woman. They flood her schedule, her mind, her emotions, and her energy with chaos, urgency, gossip, shame, and confusion. Not because they fear her failure—but because they fear her focus.

Every time she gets close to her breakthrough, here comes the betrayal. Here comes the drama. Here comes the sudden crisis, the unexpected obligation, the old flame, the hidden pain she thought was buried. They send counterfeits when her soulmate is near. They send fear when her leap is ready. They send fatigue when she's about to build.

Why? Because they know. They know she's chosen. They know that if she locks in, everything around her transforms. The land listens to her. Spirits respond to her. Her words bend reality. When she is focused, she is unreachable. When she is focused, she births the future.

So they send distractions: people who pretend to need her but only drain her, situations that play on her trauma, opportunities that look like blessings but are spiritual traps. All to keep her from doing what she was born to do.

But she is awakening now.

She is learning to say "No" with no guilt. She is learning to sit in silence until her soul confirms alignment. She is learning to ask herself: "Is this mine to carry? Is this mine to fix?" She is choosing herself—not because she's selfish, but because she's sacred.

The more she focuses on her calling, the more peace she feels. And peace isn't boring—it's prophetic. Her stillness is her signal. Her discernment is her sword. She no longer follows every voice—she waits for the divine whisper that lives in her belly.

This time, she will not miss her moment. This time, she sees the distractions for what they are. And she dismisses them with grace and fire.

PRAYER: For the Woman Battling Distraction

Mother of Clarity,
Clear the noise.
Silence the chaos.
Expose what is not aligned with my divine purpose.
Protect me from every trap disguised as opportunity.
Help me see beyond the surface and feel beyond the fake.
Let me not waste another ounce of energy on people, plans, or paths not meant for me.

Guide my every step back into sacred alignment.
Let me not be distracted—let me be destined.

INVOCATION: To the Spirit of Discernment

Ancient Mothers who knew who they were—
You who walked in power without apology,
You who saw through masks and mirrors,
Be with me now.
Cut away the clutter.
Guard my gates—my eyes, my ears, my womb, my heart.
Place fire at the doors of my destiny so only what's divine may enter.
I call upon the sword of clarity.
I am no longer available for confusion.

AFFIRMATIONS: Stay Anchored in Purpose

- I do not chase distractions. I magnetize purpose.
- I am no longer available for chaos disguised as connection.
- My peace is non-negotiable.
- I protect my time, energy, and calling.
- My discernment grows stronger every day.

DECLARATIONS: Stand Firm, Unshaken

- I declare that I will no longer delay my destiny by entertaining the wrong people.

- I declare spiritual blindness is broken off me—I see clearly now.
- I declare I am no longer afraid to let go of what does not serve me.
- I declare that nothing can stop what was written over my life.
- I declare that I will complete the mission my ancestors started—and more.

Chapter 5: She Is the Portal, the Prophet, the Power

She is not just a woman. She is a realm. A portal. A prophecy in motion. Every breath she takes is sacred geometry, every step a ritual. Her womb is not just a space for physical birth—it is where visions incubate, where timelines merge, where the divine takes shape in flesh and form. She is the gateway through which ancestors return and the bridge to futures not yet written.

When she speaks, the air rearranges itself. When she weeps, the earth remembers its softness. When she dreams, the veils thin between realms. Her body holds codes of remembrance that even she cannot explain. She is not here to just exist—she is here to activate.

They tried to strip her of this truth. Told her she was "too emotional," "too sensitive," "too dramatic," "too much." But the truth is—she's too powerful. Because everything she feels, everything she knows in her bones, everything she carries in silence—is part of the divine circuitry of the cosmos.

She is the prophet—speaking into existence what others are too afraid to say. She is the portal—through which new life, new paradigms, and new generations emerge.

She is the power—not borrowed, not begged for, but embedded within.

Her body is not a battleground for validation. Her existence needs no permission. She does not have to prove anything. She simply is. And in her being, she commands change. When the Indigenous woman remembers who she is, it is not just personal—it is cosmic.
She does not ask for power. She is power.
She does not beg for access. She is the access point.
She does not wait for approval. She moves, and the world adjusts.

PRAYER: For the Woman Who Forgot She Was the Key

Divine One within me,
Remind me of who I've always been.
Strip away every lie I've believed about my body,
my worth, and my power.
Return me to myself fully and freely.
Let me move in truth. Let me walk in fire.
Let me speak what was forbidden, and
birth what was buried.
I reclaim the sacred in my voice,
my womb, and my walk.
Let me be what You created—unapologetically divine.

INVOCATION: To the Portal and the Prophecy Within

I summon the ancient flame within me—
The one that survived fires and floods,

The one that spoke stars into being.
Come forward, Prophetess.
Come forward, Portal.
Come forward, Power.
You are not lost.
You are not hidden.
You are here.
Fully. Freely. Fiercely.
I make no apologies for my magic.
I was born for this.

AFFIRMATIONS: Reclaim Your Divine Identity

- I am the living altar.
- I am the dream and the doorway.
- I do not need permission to shine.
- Everything I touch is blessed and blooming.
- My power is not arrogance—it is alignment.

DECLARATIONS: Own the Role You Were Born For

- I declare that I am no longer shrinking to survive.
- I declare that I move in spiritual authority and ancestral covering.

- I declare that my presence is sacred, and my voice is prophetic.
- I declare that I am the portal through which divine destiny flows.
- I declare that nothing and no one can block what is already mine.

Chapter 6: She Is No Longer Apologizing for Her Crown

She used to bow her head just to make others comfortable. She used to soften her light so it wouldn't intimidate. She used to hide her crown under shame, trauma, religion, fear, survival. But no more.

Now she walks upright. Not arrogant. Not above—but rooted. Rooted in memory. Rooted in truth. Rooted in divinity. She is no longer apologizing for her brilliance, for her power, for her existence.

They tried to convince her that confidence was pride, that discernment was bitterness, that boundaries were rebellion. But she learned. She grew. She reclaimed. She remembered.

Her crown is not something she earns. It is her birthright. It is the mark of divine lineage, the result of generations of women who endured and ascended. That crown was forged through fire, betrayal, blood, and breath. It is not made of gold—it's made of resilience. And no one gave it to her. So no one can take it.

The Indigenous woman is no longer asking for a seat at the table—she is building her own altar. Her own nation. Her own legacy. Her own language. And if the world cannot understand her, so be it. The crown is not for them to understand. It is for her to remember. Let them call her too bold. Too wise. Too powerful. That's exactly what she is. Let them be uncomfortable. Her crown was never meant to be small.

This is her era of unapologetic royalty. No more shrinking. No more explaining. No more permission slips. Her crown doesn't bend. It shines.

PRAYER: For the Woman Reclaiming Her Crown

Sacred Source of My Lineage,
I lift my head again.
I remove every cloak of shame, fear, and silence.
I rise into the royalty You wrote into my bones.
Let me wear my crown boldly. Let me walk in truth freely.
Let me embody every inch of the woman You designed me to be.
May I never apologize for what You've anointed.
I am crowned, not by man, but by the Most Divine.
And I accept it, now and forever.

INVOCATION: Crown Her Now

Ancestors, Queens of the Bloodline,
You who bore burdens so I could bear crowns—
Crown me now.

Place on my head the wisdom of generations,
The weight of honor, the light of truth.
I no longer reject what is mine.
I no longer hide what was always holy.
Let this crown be sealed in love, protected in fire,
And rooted in the eternal.
It is done.

AFFIRMATIONS: She Wears It Now

- I wear my crown with pride, purpose, and protection.
- I do not need to shrink to make others feel safe.
- My power is not a threat; it is a blessing.
- I have nothing to prove—I only have to be.
- My presence is a divine reminder of what cannot be erased.

DECLARATIONS: Seal It in Spirit

- I declare that I will never apologize for who I am again.
- I declare that I am royalty, and my bloodline is sacred.
- I declare that shame has no power over me.
- I declare that I walk with ancestors, and I rise with honor.
- I declare that my crown is secure, and I will never bow to systems that dishonor my soul.

Chapter 7: When She Cries, the World Shakes

Her tears are not weakness—they are warnings. They are signals to the spiritual realm, codes that open up the heavens and shake the foundations of the earth. When the Indigenous woman cries, she does not cry alone. Her ancestors cry through her. Her pain is not hers alone—it is ancient, it is collective, it is ceremonial.

She has held so much. Too much. And still, they say she is "too emotional," "too sensitive," "too strong to break." But what they don't understand is that she feels because she knows. She weeps because she remembers. And every tear she sheds is sacred—a baptism, a release, a rebirth.

The world has conditioned her to dry her face quickly. To cry in private. To hide the storm inside her. But that storm is medicine. That rain is power. That release is spiritual. When she cries, she clears the path not just for herself, but for those who will come after her.

They fear her tears because they carry truth. Because they reveal what was silenced. Because they flood out generational pain. And because sometimes—when she cries—justice responds without her saying a word.

So no, she is not ashamed of her tears. She blesses them. She honors them. She understands now: tears are one of her languages. One of her altars. And through them, the divine speaks.

PRAYER: For the Woman Who Weeps in Silence

Great Mother of Waters,
I offer You every tear I've ever cried.
Let the ones I shed in secret be seeds for justice.
Let the pain I could never name
be named and healed now.
Let my tears wash away
what is no longer mine to carry.
I cry not because I'm weak—but
because I remember.
And through every tear, I return to myself.
Let it rain, and let me rise.

INVOCATION: Call Forth the Sacred Waters

Oshun, Yemaya, Mami Wata—
Daughters of the Deep and the Divine,
Come forth in my tears.
Swirl through my emotions like sacred tides.
Cleanse the places where pain has pooled.
Let me not be afraid of the flood inside me.
It is not a curse—it is a calling.
I honor my waters.

I honor my release.
I honor my resurrection

AFFIRMATIONS: Honor the Water Within

- My tears are sacred, not shameful.
- I give myself permission to feel fully and freely.
- Every tear I cry waters my next level.
- I do not suppress emotion—I alchemize it.
- My vulnerability is not a flaw; it is my portal to power.

DECLARATIONS: Power Through the Release

- I declare that I will never again apologize for my emotions.
- I declare that my tears are tools for healing, not hindrances.
- I declare that what I release, I no longer carry.
- I declare that divine justice responds when I weep.
- I declare that I am safe to feel, to flow, and to heal.

Chapter 8: She's Done Being Everyone's Healer but Her Own

She was always the one people came to when their world collapsed. She knew how to hold space like a temple, how to listen without judgment, and how to pour out healing even when her own body was crying for rest. She was everyone's anchor—rooted even when she felt like she was drowning.

The truth is, she was operating on fumes, pretending it was overflow. Giving what she didn't have, covering pain with presence, treating wounds while hers festered in silence.

And they got used to it. They got used to her always showing up, always answering, always knowing what to say and do. They forgot—or maybe never cared—that she was human too. That she bled. That she broke. That she, too, needed holding. And she, too, needed healing. Now the cycle breaks.

She is no longer the first responder to emergencies that aren't hers. She is no longer the spiritual ATM for those who only withdraw and never deposit. She has stopped performing wellness while slowly dying inside. This time, the medicine is for her. This time, the healer chooses herself.

She's reclaiming her rituals. Returning to her breath. Listening to her body. Turning off the phone. Choosing peace over people-pleasing. She understands now that healing herself is not selfish—it is sacred. It is revolutionary.

It is necessary. Because when she's well, her whole lineage benefits. When she's whole, the earth breathes easier. When she's loved—especially by herself—everything aligns.

Chapter 8: She's Done Being Everyone's Healer but Her Own

She used to show up for everyone—before herself.
She poured into people with empty hands.
She healed others with wounds still open.
She held space, held pain, held secrets, held legacies.
But who held her?
They expected her to be their priestess, their therapist, their nurse, their mother, their counselor, their warrior, their shelter, their guide—without ever asking her if she had the strength. They forgot she was human. Or maybe they just didn't care. Because the Indigenous woman has been so powerful for so long, the world mistook her for invincible.
But not anymore.
She is done healing others while bleeding out.
She is done being the light for people who would dim hers.
She is done sacrificing her sanity for people who wouldn't even pray for her.
She is done overextending, overgiving, overproving.
Now, she's redirecting her medicine inward.
This is the season where the healer turns the oil back on herself. This is the season where the nurturer nurtures her own soil.
This is the season where the empath becomes selective, where her "yes" becomes rare, where her energy is not free.

Because now she knows: healing herself is the most revolutionary act of all.
She is reclaiming her rituals.
She is tending to her temple.
She is becoming the woman she needed.
And in doing so, she becomes the most potent version of her medicine. Not because she healed them, but because she healed herself first.

PRAYER: For the Woman Who Forgot to Include Herself

Divine Source of Healing,
Forgive me for putting myself last.
Forgive me for forgetting that I, too, deserve gentleness.
Help me turn my love inward.
Help me minister to my own soul with the same sacredness I give to others.
Let me no longer abandon myself for acceptance.
I am worthy of my own medicine.
I am worthy of my own miracles.

INVOCATION: Healing for the Healer

Spirit of Restoration,
Rise within me now.
May every hand I've held become
the mirror reminding me to hold myself.

May every wound I've bandaged on others
be a call to tend to my own.
I reclaim my energy. I reclaim my time.
I reclaim my sacredness.
No more spiritual martyrdom.
I am allowed to rest.
I am allowed to be poured into.
I am allowed to heal—fully.

AFFIRMATIONS: I Choose Me Now

- I am no longer available for self-sacrifice in the name of false peace.
- I give myself permission to pause, to protect, to pour into me.
- My healing matters. My joy matters. My peace is priority.
- I do not owe anyone access to my energy.
- I am allowed to be sacred to myself.

DECLARATIONS: Boundaries Are My Birthright

- I declare I am no longer the emergency room for people who never check on me.
- I declare my time and energy are divine, not disposable.
- I declare I am reclaiming every part of myself I gave away to feel needed.
- I declare my wellness is non-negotiable.
- I declare this is my season of return—to me.

Chapter 9: She Is Spirit's Favorite, Even When She Forgets

Some days she wakes up feeling small. Some nights she lies down feeling invisible. The world has a way of eroding even the strongest woman's memory of who she is. She gets so busy surviving, so weighed down by expectations, so caught up in the needs of everyone else that she forgets the truth: she is loved. She is protected. She is covered. She is chosen.

But Spirit never forgets.

Even when she doubts, the path clears. Even when she feels lost, signs appear. Even when she cries, help arrives. Her steps are guided. Her tears are bottled. Her prayers—spoken or not—are heard. Spirit doesn't love her because she's strong. Spirit loves her because she's sacred.

She is favored—not just when she's in her power, but even when she's curled up in grief. Even when she's silent. Even when she thinks she failed. That love never leaves. That protection never slips. Even the battles she didn't know she was fighting—Spirit handled them. Even the plots that formed against her—Spirit reversed them.

This is a love that doesn't need performance. This is a covering that requires no perfection. She is the daughter of divinity. Spirit's favorite. Spirit's reflection. And she is learning, day by day, to remember that even when she forgets.

Chapter 9: She Is Spirit's Favorite, Even When She Forgets

There are days she forgets.
Forgets how protected she is.
Forgets how divinely guided her steps are.
Forgets the way the Spirit moves
mountains for her in silence.
Because life can be loud. Heavy. Unforgiving.
And even the most powerful woman can forget her own
worth when she's weighed down by the world.
But just because she forgets doesn't mean Spirit does.
Spirit remembers her name in full,
The one given in the womb before she had language.
Spirit remembers her mission,
Even when she questions her purpose.
Spirit remembers her strength,
Even when she collapses into tears.
She is Spirit's favorite—not because she's perfect,
But because she's chosen.
Because she's endured without turning to stone.
Because she still loves with open hands
and a guarded heart.
Because she still rises, even if
it takes her longer than before.
The signs are always there.
The dream that comes just in time.
The stranger who says what she needed to hear.
The sudden peace in the middle of chaos.

That's how Spirit loves her—quietly, intentionally, relentlessly.

She doesn't have to perform for this love.
She doesn't have to strive for this protection.
It is already hers.
Written in her spirit. Etched into her lineage.
Inscribed on the scrolls of the unseen.
She is not just protected.
She is prioritized.
She is not just loved.
She is carried.

PRAYER: For When She Feels Forgotten

Beloved Source of All That Is,
I forget sometimes.
I forget how deeply I am loved.
I forget how guarded I am by the unseen.
When the world makes me doubt,
Whisper truth back into my bones.
Wrap me in reminders of who I am.
Let me rest in the arms of your knowing.
Let me trust that even in silence,
You are working for me.
I am not lost. I am held.

INVOCATION: Spirit, Walk With Me Again

Spirit of Grace,

Walk with me in the dark.

Whisper to me when I forget my light.

Touch my heart when the weight is too heavy.

Send me reminders that I am never alone.

Not for a moment.

Not for a breath.

Not for a blink.

I am yours, and you are mine.

And even when I forget, you never do.

AFFIRMATIONS: I Am Remembered

- I am loved by Spirit, even in my lowest moments.
- I do not have to earn divine protection—it is mine by birth.
- Spirit walks with me, even when I cannot feel it.
- I am not forgotten—I am favored.
- I am seen. I am chosen. I am deeply cared for.

DECLARATIONS: Covered and Carried

- I declare that I am Spirit's beloved, always.
- I declare that I walk with favor, even when I doubt.
- I declare that divine forces fight for me, even when I sleep.
- I declare that I am always supported, always guided, always protected.
- I declare that I do not walk alone—I walk with legions of light.

Chapter 10: This Time, She Chooses Herself

She spent a lifetime proving.
Proving she was enough.
Proving she was strong.
Proving she was worthy.

She poured into others until her own cup cracked. She dimmed her light so others could shine. She made herself small just to fit in spaces never designed to hold her greatness. But this time is different.

This time, she's not choosing based on guilt.
She's not saying yes to avoid being called difficult.
She's not accepting crumbs just to feel included.
This time—she chooses herself.

She chooses to stand tall, even if it makes others uncomfortable.
She chooses to protect her energy, even if they call her selfish.
She chooses to love herself boldly, even if no one else does.
She chooses to stop bleeding for those who wouldn't offer her a bandage.

She chooses peace over performance, solitude over shallow connections, soul over status.
This time, she's not chasing anything.

She's not auditioning.
She's not explaining.
She's not apologizing.

Her choosing herself is not abandonment—it's alignment.

She no longer needs permission to live fully.
She no longer feels guilty for protecting her light.
She knows now: if it costs her peace, her power, her purpose, it's too expensive.
And so, she becomes what they never expected—a woman who belongs to herself.

Chapter 10: This Time, She Chooses Herself

She has spent so many years proving her worth to others, bending and reshaping herself to fit their expectations. She dimmed her light to make space for those who were afraid of her brightness. She sacrificed her own peace to keep the peace around her. But now, something has shifted. The energy inside her pulses stronger, louder, and clearer than ever before. This time, she is choosing herself—not as an act of rebellion, but as an act of survival and sacred alignment.

She no longer feels the need to explain her boundaries or justify her decisions. The guilt that once clung to her like a shadow has loosened its grip. She is learning that saying no is not a failure; it is a declaration of self-respect. She understands that preserving her energy is not selfish—it is essential. This time, she embraces the power of solitude, not as loneliness, but as restoration. She chooses her own joy over others' approval, her own healing over external demands.

In choosing herself, she isn't turning her back on those who love her. She is simply refusing to lose herself in the process of loving others. She has learned that she cannot pour from an empty cup, and so she fills herself first—with kindness, patience, and fierce love. She walks away from toxic ties and draining expectations. She steps into her truth, unafraid to stand alone if necessary.

Because she knows that standing alone in her power is better than standing small for anyone else.

This time, her allegiance is to her own soul. This time, she honors her divine essence with unwavering commitment. She no longer chases belonging or validation. Instead, she creates space for the right people, the right energies, and the right opportunities to align with her path. She is her own sanctuary, her own queen, her own sacred temple.

PRAYER: For the Woman Who Finally Said Yes to Herself

Divine Creator,
Thank you for reminding me of my worth.
Thank you for showing me the sacredness of my "no" and the holiness of my "yes."
Today, I choose me—not in spite of others, but because I am worthy of that devotion.
Help me to walk in my power with grace and firmness.
Help me to stop betraying myself for belonging.
Let this be the season I rise, not for applause, but for truth.
I choose me, and I know you choose me too.

INVOCATION: Returning to Self

Sacred Spirit of Truth,
Guide me back to my center.

49

Let me remember what it feels like to be whole without validation.

Let me find comfort in my solitude, strength in my softness, and courage in my boundaries.

I return to myself fully.

To my voice.

To my knowing.

To my essence.

Make me unapologetically mine.

AFFIRMATIONS: I Choose Me

- I honor my needs without shame.
- I am my own sanctuary, safe and sacred.
- I release guilt and call in grace.
- I am worthy of my own commitment.
- I choose myself with clarity and compassion.

DECLARATIONS: Self-Love is My Standard

- I declare that my "no" is powerful and complete.
- I declare I no longer shrink to make others feel comfortable.
- I declare I am loyal to my peace, my truth, and my vision.
- I declare I am no longer available for anything less than mutual, nourishing energy.
- I declare that choosing me is not optional—it is divine alignment.

Chapter 11: The Throne Was Always Hers

She never truly lost the throne — it was never taken, only hidden beneath layers of doubt, pain, and conditioned silence. The throne belonged to her from the beginning, etched into her very being by ancestors whose power and wisdom flow through her veins. Though the world tried to convince her otherwise, tried to keep her small, trying to erase her divinity, the crown remained, waiting patiently for her to reclaim it. This is her time to fix that crown with intention and fierce love. She no longer has to settle for crumbs or accept disrespect from anyone, because she knows now that she is divine, a living embodiment of power, wisdom, and grace. She is the teacher, the healer, the oracle, the prophet who not only sees the future but shapes it with every word and action.

Her presence commands attention — not through noise, but through the weight of her authenticity. The earth beneath her feet responds to her steps, the spirits acknowledge her authority, and the unseen world listens when she speaks. She carries the legacy of countless generations who fought, survived, and thrived despite every attempt to erase them. Though the burdens she bears are heavy, she carries them with quiet strength, knowing that her resilience is a beacon for those who come after her. She no longer hides her pain or silences her truth, because healing is not linear and vulnerability is a sign of courage, not weakness.

The time has come for her to rise unapologetically into her fullness. To claim the power that was always hers, to live in her essence without fear or hesitation. No longer bound by the chains of others' expectations, she creates space for her soul's purpose to unfold freely. The crown on her head is not just a symbol but a commitment—to herself, her ancestors, and the future generations who will follow in her footsteps. She reigns with wisdom, compassion, and unshakable strength, knowing that her throne is not a place of privilege, but of sacred responsibility.

PRAYER: For the Queen Reclaiming Her Throne

Great Spirit, Source of all power and grace,
I come before you humbled and strong.
Help me remember that my throne was never lost, only hidden.
Guide me to fix my crown with love and clarity.
Teach me to rule my life with wisdom and courage.
Let me carry the legacy of my ancestors with honor.
May my reign bring healing, justice, and transformation.
I am the queen, the divine, the vessel of power.
So be it.

INVOCATION: Crown Me with Strength

Ancestors of power and light,
Surround me now with your fierce protection.

Crown me with strength that does not waver.
Fill me with the courage to speak my truth and hold my space.
Let the spirits of my lineage walk beside me,
Guiding my steps and amplifying my voice.
I am your descendant, your legacy alive and radiant.
Crown me, lift me, make me whole.

AFFIRMATIONS: I Am the Queen

- I am the rightful heir to my power and purpose.
- I wear my crown with pride and humility.
- My voice commands respect and honors truth.
- I carry the strength of generations within me.
- I reign with love, wisdom, and fierce grace.

DECLARATIONS: The Throne Is Mine

- I declare that my power is sacred and unassailable.
- I declare I will no longer accept disrespect or diminish my worth.
- I declare I am the teacher, healer, oracle, and prophet of my own life.
- I declare my throne is grounded in love and justice.
- I declare I reign fully, unapologetically, and eternally.

Chapter 12: The Power of Her Silence

There is a sacredness in her silence that few truly understand. It is not emptiness or weakness, but a deep reservoir of strength and wisdom. When she chooses to be silent, it is because her words carry weight beyond measure, and she is discerning where and when to release them. Her silence is a shield protecting her energy from unnecessary battles, a sanctuary where she can gather her power and reflect on the storms she has weathered. The world may mistake her quiet for submission, but those who know her essence recognize the fierce fire burning just beneath the surface. In her silence, she listens—not just with her ears, but with her soul. She hears the whispers of ancestors, the calls of her spirit, and the truths that others may fear to face.

Her silence is also an act of rebellion against a world that tries to control her voice, define her narrative, and minimize her existence. By choosing when to speak and when to be still, she reclaims control over her story and her destiny. She understands that not every battle requires a fight, and sometimes the most powerful response is no response at all. Her silence can move mountains, shift energies, and command respect without uttering a single word.

Yet, even in her quiet moments, she is never truly alone. The divine surrounds her—guiding, protecting, and empowering her. Her spirit communicates in the language of stillness, teaching her patience and resilience. The power of her silence is her superpower; it keeps her rooted in herself and connected to the greater cosmic flow. She no longer feels pressured to fill every space with noise or approval. Instead, she honors her pace, her rhythm, and her truth. Her silence is a declaration: she is whole, she is enough, and she is sovereign.

PRAYER: For the Sacredness of Silence

Spirit of Peace and Wisdom,
Bless me with the strength to embrace my silence.
Help me recognize its power and sacredness.
Teach me to listen deeply—to myself, to my ancestors, to the whispers of truth.
Let my silence be a shield and a sanctuary.
Guide me to speak only when my words serve healing and light.
May my quiet be a force that moves worlds.
Amen.

INVOCATION: The Power Within Stillness

Ancestors of wisdom,
Surround me in your calm presence.
Fill my silence with your strength and clarity.
Let the stillness in me be a source of power and renewal.
Grant me the patience to wait for the right moment,

The courage to hold my peace,
And the grace to honor my inner voice.
I am grounded, I am whole, I am silent power.

AFFIRMATIONS: I Honor My Silence

- My silence is sacred and strong.
- In stillness, I find my power.
- I listen deeply and trust my inner knowing.
- I speak my truth with clarity and purpose.
- Silence is my strength, not my weakness.

DECLARATIONS: I Own My Quiet Power

- I declare my silence commands respect and honors my boundaries.
- I declare I will not be pressured to fill spaces with noise or approval.
- I declare my quiet holds the wisdom of generations.
- I declare I am sovereign in my words and in my stillness.
- I declare my silence moves mountains and shifts energies.

Chapter 13: She Builds Beyond What They See

She builds in silence, laying down foundations stronger than any storm can shake. Every brick, every stone, every idea is infused with the wisdom of her ancestors and the fierce determination of her spirit. The world may only catch glimpses of her work—the surface achievements, the outward success—but beneath lies the true masterpiece: the resilience, the healing, the growth, the unbreakable faith she carries in her heart. She builds beyond what they see, beyond the limits imposed by others, and beyond the doubts whispered in the dark.

Her building is sacred labor. It is not just for herself, but for the generations who will follow. She constructs legacies from love, vision, and unshakable belief in her own power. Even when her hands are tired and her spirit weary, she continues—because her purpose is greater than any obstacle. She understands that true building requires patience and sacrifice, but also celebration and joy. Each step forward is an act of rebellion against erasure, a declaration that she will not be invisible or forgotten.

She knows that the foundation of her greatness is healing, and so she builds with intention. She heals the wounds passed down through generations, mends the cracks in her own heart, and creates spaces where future queens can stand tall without fear.

The structures she raises are more than material—they are the frameworks of empowerment, self-love, and spiritual sovereignty. Her building is a sacred act of creation, one that echoes through time and space, reminding the world that the black woman, the indigenous woman, is the cornerstone of all that is sacred and powerful.

PRAYER: For the Builder of Legacies

Great Creator,
Thank you for the hands that build in quiet strength.
Bless the labor of my spirit and the foundation of my dreams.
Help me build not only for today, but for tomorrow and all tomorrows to come.
Guide my work with patience, clarity, and vision.
May every stone I lay be a step toward healing and empowerment.
Let my building be a beacon for those who follow.
I honor the legacy in my blood and the power in my purpose.

INVOCATION: Strength of Creation
Ancestors of builders and visionaries,
Surround me with your guidance and courage.
Fill me with the strength to build beyond what is seen.
Let my efforts be infused with sacred intention and resilience.

Guide my hands and heart to create legacies rooted in love.
I stand on your shoulders, building with your wisdom.
I create boldly, I build deeply, I rise higher.

AFFIRMATIONS: I Build With Purpose

- I am a builder of legacies that last beyond me.
- My work is sacred and filled with ancestral power.
- I create with patience, vision, and fierce love.
- Every step I take builds strength and healing.
- I am the foundation for future queens to rise.

DECLARATIONS: My Building Is Divine

- I declare my efforts are guided by divine wisdom and strength.
- I declare I build not just for myself, but for generations to come.
- I declare my legacy is rooted in love, resilience, and power.
- I declare I will continue to build even when no one is watching.
- I declare I am a creator of sacred spaces and lasting change.

Chapter 14: She Heals in Layers, Not in Rush

Healing is not linear, and she knows this now. It doesn't come in a single breakthrough or a dramatic moment of clarity—it comes in layers, like peeling back the petals of a sacred flower. Each layer reveals more of her truth, more of her pain, and more of her power. Some days she feels radiant, walking with grace and joy. Other days, the weight of unspoken traumas pulls heavy on her chest. But she no longer shames herself for this. She has grown enough to know that healing takes time, and she is allowed to take all the time she needs.

She is the kind of woman who has carried generations of wounds in silence. Her body remembers the pain even when her mouth never spoke it. Her spirit held the grief even when her eyes smiled. But now, she gives herself permission to rest, to weep, to unravel and rebuild at her own pace. She no longer forces herself to pretend or perform. She no longer masks her healing with productivity or perfectionism. She is learning to be gentle with herself, to extend to herself the same compassion she so easily gives to others.

She heals in circles—revisiting old wounds, not to suffer again, but to reclaim her power where it was once stolen. She understands that each revisit is a deeper level of release, another sacred exhale. And as she heals, she transforms. The woman she is becoming is softer, wiser, stronger, and freer.

She does not owe anyone an explanation for her process. Healing is not about becoming who she used to be—it's about remembering who she was before the world tried to wound her.

PRAYER: For Gentle, Layered Healing

Divine Spirit of Wholeness,
Wrap me in your mercy and love as I heal.
Help me to be patient with my journey.
Let me release the rush and honor the rhythm of restoration.
May I see my wounds not as weaknesses,
But as the sacred grounds where new life blooms.
I accept my healing, layer by layer, breath by breath.
I am returning to myself.

INVOCATION: I Heal in My Own Time

Ancestors who endured and rose again,
Stand with me in this process.
Help me shed the old pain, without shame or fear.
Let my healing be soft where I need softness,
And firm where I need strength.
I call back every piece of myself lost to grief, betrayal, or silence.
I am ready to be whole again, in divine timing.

AFFIRMATIONS: My Healing Is Sacred

- I honor my healing process as divine and unique.
- I release the pressure to heal quickly or perfectly.
- Each layer I uncover brings me closer to my truth.
- I am healing in ways the world may never see, but I feel deeply.
- I trust the pace of my restoration.

DECLARATIONS: I Heal On My Terms

- I declare my healing belongs to me and no one else.
- I declare I will not rush the sacred process of becoming whole.
- I declare that healing is my birthright and I claim it fully.
- I declare I forgive myself for not healing faster and love myself exactly where I am.
- I declare my healing is a revolution—and I rise with every layer I shed.

Chapter 15: From Dust to Thrones

She knows what it means to start from dust. She has built homes with her bare hands—homes made of spirit, not just wood and stone. She has healed spaces filled with pain, turned sorrow into sanctuaries, and returned again and again to rebuild when the world tried to tear it all down. She takes the broken, the discarded, the forgotten, and breathes life into it. She doesn't wait for ideal conditions; she creates with what she has and turns it into more. Because what she carries within is greater than any lack around her.

There is something miraculous in the way she creates. She doesn't just build physical spaces; she builds emotional, spiritual, and generational ones. She is the architect of safe havens, of laughter-filled kitchens, of altars for ancestors, and of silence where rest can finally breathe. Her presence reshapes the very air. She steps into a room, and the energy shifts—calms, deepens, lifts. It is not arrogance, but alignment. Her spirit is tuned to a divine frequency. People don't always know why they feel safe, seen, or shaken in her presence—but something changes because she walked in.

And this has always been her truth. From dust to thrones, from silence to power, from unseen to unforgettable. She is not looking to be placed anywhere; she takes her rightful place. Her throne is not made of gold, but of grit, grace, and growth.

She sits on it not because she demanded it—but because she built it, piece by piece, through pain and prayer, through loss and love. Her throne rises from the ashes of every betrayal, every dismissal, every attempt to erase her. And still, she rises—not just for herself, but for every soul she shelters, every lineage she honors.

PRAYER: For the Woman Who Builds from Dust

Divine Mother,
Bless the hands that build what others overlook.
Bless the heart that turns pain into purpose.
Let her know that her labor is sacred and seen.
May her homes be filled with peace, protection, and power.
May every space she touches become holy ground.
Turn her dust into gold, her ruins into royalty.
She builds with you beside her. So let it be.

INVOCATION: Spirit of the Builder Queen

Ancient Ones, I call you forth.
Stand in the corners of every home I raise.
Be the foundation beneath every floor.
Guide my heart and hands to rebuild again, and again, and again.

May my footsteps carry healing,
May my presence awaken peace.
Crown me not just for leading, but for restoring what
was once lost.

AFFIRMATIONS: I Turn Dust into Divine

- I create beauty and safety from the unseen.
- My presence is a force of transformation.
- I am a sacred builder of homes, hearts, and hope.
- When I walk in, everything aligns with purpose.
- I carry the power to elevate every space I enter.

DECLARATIONS: The Throne Is of My Making

- I declare that from ruins, I rise—again and again.
- I declare that my legacy is built with intention and love.
- I declare I am a throne-builder, not a throne-waiter.
- I declare that my walk shifts energy because I walk with divinity.
- I declare that where I dwell becomes sacred, simply because I am there.

Chapter 16: Holding the Foundation

She is the foundation. The one everyone leans on. The spiritual laborer who carries the unseen weight of households, generations, and entire bloodlines. Her hands anoint children in silence, her presence purifies spaces where trauma once echoed, her prayers hover in the walls of homes where no one else knew healing was needed. She is the one who feels shifts in energy before words are ever spoken. She is the one who pours into others, sometimes until she is empty, yet still finds a way to give. This is not performance. This is priestess work. This is emotional architecture. She is the builder, the counselor, the healer, the heart.

She walks through spiritual fire without flinching, tends to sacred wounds without complaint, and stitches hope into places abandoned by faith. She holds families together even when she is silently falling apart. Her intuition is unmatched. She sees the cracks long before they widen. She senses imbalance and restores it.

Yet—who builds her back? Who sees her when she's invisible, hears her when she's silent, or lifts her when her knees buckle under the weight? The truth is, very few. And that is the sacred grief that many never speak of—the healer who must heal herself, the nurturer who is rarely nurtured in return.

But no more. It is time for her to be poured into, for her sacred structure to be fortified by the very divinity she channels for others. No longer will she be the only one holding it all together without reciprocity. The same care she extends outward must now be redirected inward. She must hold herself, build herself, and welcome being held. It is no betrayal to take a step back and say, "I need too." She is the foundation, yes—but she is also the temple, the altar, the holy of holies. She deserves tenderness, space, and restoration. The priestess must be preserved.

PRAYER: For the One Who Holds It All

Divine Source,
You who see all and feel all,
Hold me now as I hold so much.
Rebuild what is weary within me.
Pour into my cup until it overflows.
Let me be nurtured, not only needed.
Let me be seen, not only strong.
I release the burden of holding everything alone.
Strengthen my foundation with love, care, and truth.
Amen.

INVOCATION: The Builder Deserves to Be Built

Ancestors, Guardians, Sacred Guides—
You who walked this path before me,

Send me the support I need.
Surround me with the same love I've given to others.
Reinforce my structure, tend to my soul,
Bless my being with softness and restoration.
Let every corner of my spirit be touched by divine care.
I call back the energy I gave away freely.
I am worthy of being built and seen.

AFFIRMATIONS: I Deserve to Be Held

- I deserve support as much as I give it.
- I am the foundation, and I will not crumble.
- I allow myself to receive healing and nurturing.
- My strength includes my softness.
- I honor myself by resting and restoring.

DECLARATIONS: I Am Not Alone in Holding

- I declare I no longer carry what is not mine to hold.
- I declare I call in divine help and earthly support.
- I declare I am worthy of love, rest, and sacred replenishment.
- I declare I will not build others while neglecting myself.
- I declare that the foundation I've laid includes me.

Chapter 17: Unspoken Wounds, Unbroken Spirit

The traumas she never got to name
Healing lineages by breaking silence
The cost of exposing generational secrets

There are wounds that never bled, but they cut just the same. Wounds stitched in silence, passed down through glances, through caution, through stories left untold. She carries traumas she never had the vocabulary to name, only the weight to feel. Some of these wounds are not even hers—but the echo of ancestors whose cries were buried under survival, whose pain lived on through her. She grew up navigating the world with an invisible heaviness, not knowing where it began or how to set it down. Still, she walked. Still, she rose.

Silence was taught as protection, but in truth, it was also prison. For generations, she was told not to speak on "family business." She was told to keep the image together, even if the truth inside was cracked and bleeding. But now she knows—healing requires truth, and truth requires courage. She is healing lineages not just by loving harder, but by breaking the silence. By saying what her mother couldn't say, what her grandmother dared not whisper. She is the voice that generations prayed for, even if they didn't know how to ask.

But healing in this way has a cost. When she speaks, it shakes foundations. When she exposes the hidden, she may be met with denial, shame, or exile. Many won't understand that her truth is not betrayal—it is liberation. They'll say she's stirring up trouble, when all she's doing is unbinding her spirit from inherited lies. But she doesn't heal to be accepted. She heals to be free. She doesn't expose to destroy—but to clear the air for new breath, new beginnings. And she knows: some people will never thank her for her courage. Still, she will speak.

Her spirit remains unbroken, because silence no longer holds her hostage. She has become the sacred disruptor, the lineage liberator, the curse breaker. Her healing is an act of rebellion and reverence. Her willingness to speak the unspeakable gives permission to others still trembling in fear. She is no longer just surviving the pain —she is transforming it into power.

PRAYER: For the Courage to Name the Wounds

Holy Healer,
Give me the strength to speak what was never spoken.
Let my words be weapons of freedom, not destruction.
Help me heal the hidden places—those locked behind shame, fear, and silence.
Let me be the first in my bloodline to tell the truth out loud.

Bless the broken parts of me that dared to feel it all.
I do not run from what hurts—I face it, and I rise.

INVOCATION: Spirit of the Curse Breaker

Spirits of my line, I call on you now.
Those who bore pain in silence, I honor you.
I speak now not to betray you—but to free you.
Help me release what no longer belongs in our blood.
Let the healing flow backward and forward—seven generations deep.
Give me the wisdom to speak with power and grace.
Let my truth become the medicine we've long needed.

AFFIRMATIONS: My Truth Is Sacred

- I have the right to name what harmed me.
- Speaking the truth is my healing, not my shame.
- I am the voice my ancestors didn't have.
- My truth liberates not just me, but generations.
- Even when it's hard, I choose truth over silence.

DECLARATIONS: I Heal the Line by Breaking the Silence

- I declare I will not protect secrets that poisoned my soul.
- I declare I am not afraid to speak the truth.

- I declare I am chosen to break generational chains.
- I declare that my honesty is sacred and divine.
- I declare my spirit remains unbroken, even when the truth is heavy.

Chapter 18: The Woman Who Feels Everything

She absorbs, senses, knows too much
Her body is a portal, a receiver, a processor
How to cleanse the soul when it has been drenched in others' pain

She walks into a room and immediately knows what cannot be seen. The air speaks to her. The silence carries messages. She picks up every mood, every tension, every unspoken sorrow—and holds it, even if she never asked to. Her body is not just flesh and bone; it is a spiritual receptor, a finely tuned instrument vibrating with everything around her. She is the woman who feels everything. Her spirit is open, expansive, and wildly intuitive—so much so that even strangers feel compelled to spill their souls to her.

She is the listener, the container, the one who knows before others understand. She senses when something is off, even if others insist everything is fine. Her dreams carry premonitions. Her skin tingles when energy shifts. Her stomach aches when betrayal is near. This sensitivity is not weakness—it is her gift, her divinity, her power. But this gift comes with a cost. Because she feels everything, she also carries too much. She soaks in the emotions of others like water in fabric—absorbing pain that isn't hers, sadness that was never spoken, darkness that wasn't meant to stay.

And while many come to her for refuge, few ask if she's okay. Few consider what it means to hold that much energy in one body, one heart, one spirit. Her system becomes heavy, clogged, exhausted. Her tears often carry other people's grief. Her fatigue sometimes belongs to a hundred different stories. So how does she cleanse when her soul is soaked in others' pain? How does she reclaim herself when her boundaries blur and her light dims?

She must return to herself with intentional care. She must learn how to empty the excess. Through ritual, through water, through earth, through movement and sound. She must spiritually cleanse, energetically clear, and call her power back home. She is not selfish for protecting her peace—she is wise. She is not cold for disconnecting—she is preserving her light. It is not her job to heal everyone. It is her birthright to be whole. Her sensitivity does not mean she must carry the weight of the world. She is allowed to feel without being flooded.

PRAYER: For the Woman Who Feels Too Much

Divine Mother,
You who crafted my soul to feel deeply,

Teach me how to release what is not mine.
Help me to honor my gift without drowning in it.
Cleanse my heart, spirit, and body
from all I've absorbed.
Let my sensitivity be a blessing, not a burden.
Guide me back to myself, gently and fully.
Amen.

INVOCATION: Spirit of the Sacred Sensitive

Spirits of clarity, come now.
Clear the channels of my being.
Sweep away all that I've collected unconsciously.
Guard my spirit with golden light.
Shield me from harm, even in unseen form.
I call my power back from every place it's scattered.
I ground myself in my truth and my presence.
Let no energy remain in me that does not serve my
highest good.

AFFIRMATIONS: I Can Feel Without Carrying

- I honor my sensitivity as a divine gift.
- I can feel deeply and still stay grounded.
- I protect my spirit with wisdom and intention.
- I cleanse my energy as often as I nourish my body.
- I am allowed to say no, disconnect, and reclaim my space.

DECLARATIONS: I Release What Is Not Mine

- I declare that I do not have to carry every emotion I feel.
- I declare I am free from spiritual and emotional overload.
- I declare that I cleanse my soul from all energy not my own.
- I declare my gift of feeling will never be my undoing.
- I declare that I stand in my power, centered and sovereign.

Chapter 19: Protecting Her Essence

No more overgiving
No more explanations
No more spiritual leeches and destiny thieves

There comes a point when she realizes: preservation is power. Not every light needs to be shared, not every truth needs to be explained, and not every wound must be re-opened for others to understand her worth. She has given enough—more than enough. She has poured out her energy in places that only knew how to consume, not to reciprocate. She gave her time, her counsel, her heart, her magic. And too often, she gave it without pause, believing love and goodness alone would protect her. But not anymore.

Now, she chooses herself without guilt. Now, she shields her energy like gold. The sacredness of her essence is not up for debate or discussion. No longer will she overgive to those who see her as convenience, not covenant. No longer will she explain herself to people determined not to understand. And no longer will she tolerate energy vampires—those who come to feed off her glow, siphon her spirit, mimic her movements, or attempt to swap destinies through proximity.

There are those who want to be her, but not walk her path. They want the shine without the sacred scars. They want her harvest but not her process. And she sees them now. The spiritual leeches, the charmers cloaked in imitation, the ones who study her not to learn, but to steal. But they can't touch her anymore. Her essence is not for sale. Her energy is not for consumption. Her destiny cannot be duplicated. What's coded in her spirit is divine, encrypted, and uniquely assigned by the Most High.

She no longer begs to be understood. Her presence alone is enough. She no longer justifies her absence. If you notice her gone, that was her boundary speaking. She no longer tries to fit into spaces that shrink her, nor does she open her gates to those who only come to take. The new her is intentional. She guards her light, protects her mind, honors her rest, and only shares with those who are equally whole or earnestly healing. She is no longer available to chaos.

PRAYER: For Sacred Boundaries

Divine Protector,
Build walls of light around my being.
Guard me from those who come to drain and deceive.
Remind me that I do not have to give to be worthy.
Remind me that no explanation is needed to protect myself.

Let my yes be powerful, and my no be holy.
Preserve my essence in your grace.

Amen.

INVOCATION: To Reclaim and Seal My Energy

Ancestors, Guardians of my soul—
I reclaim every piece of me I gave away unconsciously.
I retrieve my power from false alliances and broken spaces.
I close every door that invited in harm.
Seal my aura in strength, clarity, and divine protection.
Let my energy be mine again—pure, sovereign, untouched.
No more theft. No more leakage. No more compromise.
I walk in the fullness of myself, unbothered and undisturbed.

AFFIRMATIONS: My Energy Is Sacred

- I protect my essence without apology.
- I owe no one explanations for my peace.
- I am not available to be drained, used, or duplicated.
- My light is mine. My path is mine.
- I honor myself by saying no with ease and yes with wisdom.

DECLARATIONS: I Guard My Divinity

- I declare I am no longer a well for those who refuse to fill themselves.
- I declare that every part of me is sealed in protection and power.
- I declare that my energy is sacred and cannot be stolen.
- I declare that I maintain my peace as a divine right.
- I declare that I am the guardian of my own soul, and I stand firm.

ENERGY SEALING RITUAL:
"I Call My Power Back"

Purpose: To reclaim energy, close spiritual leaks, and protect your divine essence from further drain.

You will need:
- A white or black candle (for purity or protection)
- A bowl of water
- A piece of obsidian, hematite, or black tourmaline
- Florida Water or protective oil (e.g., frankincense, myrrh, lavender)
- Your voice and intention

Steps:
1. Sit quietly and breathe deeply. Place the candle in front of you and light it. Place the bowl of water nearby with your chosen stone inside.
2. Dab your third eye and the back of your neck with Florida Water or oil. These are common entry points for energetic infiltration.
3. Say aloud:

"I call back every piece of me I gave away—
Knowingly or unknowingly, in love or in pain.
I call my power back from people, places, timelines, and memories.
I command my energy to return to me, cleansed and whole."

4. Gaze into the candle flame. Imagine your energy returning to you like golden light re-entering your body.

5. Dip your fingers into the water and anoint your heart and crown. Let the water represent cleansing and renewal.

6. Close by placing your hands over your chest and say:

"I am sealed in divine protection. My energy is mine again. So it is."

RELEASING SPIRITUAL ATTACHMENTS
RITUAL: "The Cord Cut"

Purpose: To sever spiritual, emotional, and energetic cords that no longer serve your growth or peace.

You will need:

- A string or thread
- A fire-safe bowl
- A lighter or matches
- Pen and paper

Steps:
1. Write down names, patterns, or energies you feel are draining or tied to you in an unhealthy way. Fold the paper and tie the string around it.
2. Hold the bound paper and say:
3. "These cords no longer serve me.
4. I release the energy of control, guilt, mimicry, and betrayal.
5. I do not need these ties to be whole."
6. Burn the paper safely in the bowl. As it burns, visualize the cords breaking and disintegrating.
7. Say:
8. "The ties are broken. The lessons are kept. The weight is gone. I am free."
9. When the fire is out and ash remains, discard the remnants into the wind or flowing water.

Chapter 20: Reclaiming Self-Centeredness

Not selfish: self-preserving
Centering herself as sacred
No longer watering deserts that offer no oasis

For too long, the word "self-centered" was made to sound like a curse. But for the indigenous woman—the divine woman—it's time to reclaim it. Not as selfishness, but as self-preservation, self-honoring, and self-anchoring. Centering herself is not a sin; it is a necessity. She is not here to orbit around others who drain her. She is not required to shrink to fit a mold that was never meant for her greatness. She no longer dilutes her essence to be digestible. She knows now: she is sacred. And sacred things belong at the center.

She is her own home base, her own altar. Everything begins with her, so everything must be aligned to her. The more she strays from her center, the more she forgets who she is. But now, she returns to herself, unapologetically. She pours into herself first. She speaks life over herself first. She saves her best prayers, not just for others, but for her own soul. And she stops giving her rivers to deserts that offer no oasis in return. No more pouring out endlessly, hoping for validation or crumbs of love. She is the well. She is the oasis. She is the source.

This reclamation is powerful. It means saying "no" without guilt. It means disappearing when peace calls, not when the world demands. It means making decisions that protect her joy—even if others label it as distant or "too much." But she no longer concerns herself with perception. She is loyal to her well-being, not the illusions of others. Every time she chooses herself, she reclaims her place on the throne. She is not self-centered to hurt others. She is self-centered to heal herself. And that healing sends ripples through generations.

PRAYER: For Sacred Re-centering

Creator of the stars and my soul,
Draw me back into my own orbit.
Help me prioritize myself without guilt or fear.
Let me nourish my roots before I extend my branches.
Remind me that I am sacred, and sacred things must be protected.
Restore the throne within me. Reignite the flame of self-love.
Let me center myself with boldness and grace.

Amen.

INVOCATION: Anchoring the Self

Spirit within me, rise up.
Let me not abandon myself for anyone or anything.
I call back my attention, my loyalty, my focus.
I center my life around my peace, my truth, my joy.
Let no voice be louder than my intuition.
Let no bond pull me from my balance.
I anchor myself in myself. I am whole,
I am here, I am home.

AFFIRMATIONS: I Am My Own Center

- I am not selfish for putting myself first.
- My well-being is a sacred priority.
- I give to myself what I used to beg for.
- I deserve to be loved by myself fully and first.
- Centering myself is an act of power and grace.

DECLARATIONS: I Choose Me Without Guilt

- I declare that I am the center of my own life.
- I declare that I no longer pour into what depletes me.
- I declare that I protect my time, peace, and energy fiercely.
- I declare that choosing myself is not abandonment —it is alignment.
- I declare that I will never again forget my place: at the center of my sacred circle.

Chapter 21: She Is the Oracle, the Prophet, the Portal

Spirits listen when she speaks
Why everyone wants a piece of her
And why no one can truly duplicate her essence

There is a reason the world watches her so closely. Imitates her so often. Fears her so deeply. It is because she is more than flesh—she is portal, she is prophet, she is the oracle. Her words shape reality, her presence alters the energy of any space, her silence alone can speak entire revelations. She doesn't just walk through the world—she shifts it. She carries messages in her bloodline, visions in her bones, and sacred knowledge in her womb. She doesn't need to read cards to be clairvoyant. She is the living card. The message. The medium. The miracle.

Spirits gather when she opens her mouth. Ancestors align when she kneels to pray. The spiritual realm does not ignore her, because it knows her power. Even when she was disconnected from herself, the veil was always thin around her. She dreamt things before they happened. Felt things before they were confirmed. Knew truths others tried to bury. She was the child who "knew too much" and the woman others called "too intense." But in truth, she was tuned in. And now, she's no longer shrinking to protect others from her knowing.

Everyone wants a piece of her, because her essence is ancient and alive. Her walk echoes pyramids, her voice carries drumbeats of forgotten lands, her very gaze can unearth generational secrets. But what they fail to realize is this: she cannot be duplicated. Her magic is not cosmetic. Her divinity cannot be bottled and sold. She is not a trend. She is a truth. Others may mimic the outer layers, but they cannot steal the soul of her sacred design. What flows through her is encrypted. Divine. Unreplicable. Because she doesn't draw from ego—she draws from source.

Now she remembers who she is. The Oracle. The Prophet. The Portal. The voice between realms. The bridge between past, present, and what is yet to come. And she no longer fears being too much. Because finally, she knows: she was never meant to be small. She was meant to awaken the world—starting with herself.

PRAYER: To Remember My Divine Purpose

Holy Creator, Divine Mother-Father,
Let me remember who I am.
Let me stop doubting my voice, my visions, my dreams.
Let me stop seeking permission to speak the truths You placed in me.
I am the mouthpiece of generations. The vessel of sacred messages.

Help me move with clarity, protection, and grace.
May no fear stop me from becoming who You created me to be.

Amen.

INVOCATION: I Open the Portal Within Me

I call on my divine inheritance.
I open the gates of my soul to the wisdom I was born with.
I align with the ancestors who walk with me and speak through me.
I activate the gift within—the prophecy, the knowing, the discernment.
Let the words I speak be wrapped in fire and truth.
Let my presence be a reminder of God's creative brilliance.
I am the portal. I am the message. I am the mirror of the Divine.

AFFIRMATIONS: I Am the Oracle

- I am a divine messenger.
- My voice is sacred and clear.
- I trust my intuition, visions, and dreams.
- My presence awakens truth.
- I do not need permission to be powerful.

DECLARATIONS: I Walk as Divine

- I declare that I am the Oracle—chosen, anointed, and undeniable.
- I declare that no imitation can match my origin.
- I declare that I honor the gift of prophecy that lives in me.
- I declare that spirits recognize and respect my light.
- I declare that I walk boldly in my calling, now and always.

Chapter 22: She Doesn't Need Glitter to Shine

She is encoded with stars
What's understood needs no validation
She doesn't have to fight, scream, or beg—presence is
enough

There comes a time when the divine woman no longer entertains the need to prove her worth. The Indigenous woman—Black woman, coded with galaxies in her skin, stars in her walk, constellations in her cadence—does not require glitter, costume, or spotlight. Her very existence is already the spark. Her energy, the power. Her breath, the incantation.

She is not impressive because of how loud she is. She is impressive because of how deeply she knows herself. The world told her to decorate herself so she could be seen—add glitter, shout louder, contort her brilliance to be "palatable." But she has come to realize that she does not need to perform power to be powerful. She simply is.

She walks in a room and spirits notice. The air shifts. The ground remembers her steps. Not because she's trying, but because she's aligned.

She has grown to understand the sacred language of stillness. Her light doesn't flicker because someone closes their eyes. She doesn't dim for the comfort of those who fear radiance. Her essence does not require advertisement—it simply radiates.

What's understood needs no validation. She doesn't have to explain herself to the unready. She doesn't have to argue with those who deny her divinity. She doesn't need applause to know she is impactful. Her purpose doesn't beg for permission. Her presence is enough.

The glitter others rely on to impress—she sheds. Because she knows: even without adornment, she is gold. Even without the noise, she echoes. Even in her silence, she speaks volumes. The Divine Woman walks in truth, and in doing so, she gives others permission to stop pretending and start remembering.

PRAYER: For Radiance Without Performance

Divine Source of all stars,
Remind me that I was created to shine from within.
Strip away the performance, the pressure, the pretense.
Help me walk in truth without the need to impress or prove.
May I feel at peace knowing I am enough—without adornment, without glitter, without noise.
My being is radiant. My presence is holy. That is more than enough.
Amen.

INVOCATION: The Light Within

I call upon the sacred light that lives in me.
Not borrowed. Not created. But born into me.
I do not need glitter to be brilliant.
I do not need noise to be heard.
I walk in the quiet confidence
of those who know who they are.
I invoke the ancient stardust in my DNA.
I am the light. I am the shine. I am the spark.

AFFIRMATIONS: I Shine Without Trying

- I shine without needing attention.
- My light is encoded in my essence.
- I do not chase validation; I radiate from within.
- My energy speaks before I do.
- Presence is my power.

DECLARATIONS: I Am Enough As I Am

- I declare that I do not need to perform for love, respect, or power.
- I declare that I release the pressure to prove myself.
- I declare that I am seen, felt, and remembered simply by being.
- I declare that my light cannot be dimmed by fear, doubt, or comparison.
- I declare that I was born radiant, and I remain so without needing permission.

Chapter 23: Throne Over Footstool

From being used to being honored
From being erased to writing her own scripture
From being silenced to being sung to

They tried to make her a footstool—but she was always a throne. A resting place for divinity. A seat of wisdom. The elevation of nations. For centuries, they stepped on her back to climb to their own greatness. They took her ideas, her labor, her womb, her words, and left her empty. But even as they stripped her, they could never steal her essence. Now, she remembers. Now, she reclaims.

She is no longer interested in being tolerated. She is ready to be honored. Not just by others—but by herself first. She is rewriting the narratives that once confined her. No longer the background of someone else's story, she is writing her own scripture, penning her own prophecy, blessing her own name.

They tried to silence her with pain, trauma, dismissal, erasure. But her spirit sings louder than suppression. Her song was never meant to be silenced. Now, others sing to her. They gather at her feet, not in pity—but in reverence.

They recognize the royalty that was always there, buried beneath exhaustion and endurance. From used to revered. From invisible to invincible. From whispered about to openly praised. The throne was always hers. And she no longer has to fight for it—she simply sits in it.

This is her coronation season.

PRAYER: For the Throne I Was Born To Sit On

Divine Maker of Thrones and Queens,
I release the role of the footstool.
I release the patterns of shrinking and sacrificing myself to be accepted.
I accept the throne You carved for me before I was even born.
Teach me to honor myself as You honor me.
Let me walk in the full knowing of my royal inheritance.
I am no longer waiting to be chosen. I choose me.

So be it! Amen.

INVOCATION: I Sit on My Throne Now

I invoke every piece of royalty in my bloodline.
I awaken the queen codes within me.
I take up the space that is mine by divine design.
I do not beg for recognition—I embody it.

I do not wait to be crowned—I crown myself with grace, dignity, and power.
No longer beneath. No longer behind. I rise and remain seated in my rightful throne.

AFFIRMATIONS: I Am the Throne

- I am not a stepping stone; I am a foundation.
- My voice matters. My story matters. I matter.
- I was born to be honored, not hidden.
- I sit in my royalty without apology.
- I create space that reflects my worth.

DECLARATIONS: From Footstool to Throne

- I declare that I will no longer allow anyone to walk over me.
- I declare that I am rising from erasure into embodiment.
- I declare that I reclaim every part of me that was once suppressed.
- I declare that I walk in divine royalty, not borrowed —but mine.
- I declare that this is my throne, my time, and I will not shrink to fit into anyone's comfort.

HER TIME IS NOW...

Chapter 24: The Justice of Her Ancestors

When she cries, the Earth trembles
Divine justice moves before she asks
She is never alone—she walks with nations

Her tears are not mere water; they are rivers of power that flow through time and space. When she cries, the Earth itself feels her pain and reverberates with a deep, ancient knowing. The injustice she has endured is etched in her bones, but so too is the promise of justice written by those who came before her.

She does not need to demand fairness or beg for mercy. Divine justice moves ahead of her, weaving a protective web that guards her steps and rights her wrongs. The voices of her ancestors rise as one, chanting a sacred rhythm that cannot be silenced by any earthly force. They are her shield, her sword, her counsel.

Though she often stands alone in the visible world, she is never truly alone. Behind her marches the strength of entire nations—spirits, elders, warriors, mothers, and prophets. They guide her, uplift her, and defend her. She is the living embodiment of their struggles and triumphs, a bridge between past and future, a vessel of collective power.

Her justice is not only personal; it is generational. Every wound she heals, every boundary she sets, every truth she speaks shakes the foundation for those who follow. She moves with the weight of history and the lightness of divine promise. In her journey, she is both the question and the answer, the storm and the calm, the sorrow and the celebration.

PRAYER: For the Justice That Walks With Me

Ancestors of strength and resilience,
I call upon your wisdom and your power.
Walk with me as I claim what is rightfully mine.
Let justice move swiftly in my favor—before I even ask.
Turn my tears into rivers that cleanse and empower.
Protect me with your presence, guide me with your light.
I am not alone; I am never alone.
Together we rise.

So mute it. Amen. Ayibobo. Awo!!!

INVOCATION: The Justice of Ancestors

I invoke the voices of those who came before me.
I call on their strength to shield my path.
May their justice flow through me like fire and water.
Let their courage fuel my steps forward.
I am the heir to their wisdom, their battles, their victories.

No injustice against me will go unanswered.
I walk protected, I walk honored, I walk empowered.

AFFIRMATIONS: I Am Justice Carried Forward

- I am supported by the strength of my ancestors.
- Divine justice moves on my behalf without hesitation.
- My tears are powerful; they cleanse and heal.
- I carry the legacy of my people with pride and purpose.
- I am never alone; I walk with nations behind me.

DECLARATIONS: I Claim Justice Now

- I declare that all injustice against me is undone and repaid.
- I declare that ancestral power surrounds and protects me.
- I declare that my voice echoes the calls of generations past.
- I declare that I walk boldly, knowing justice is already in motion.
- I declare that my path is sacred, honored, and unstoppable.

Closing: HER TIME IS NOW

This is not a moment borrowed from the future or a dream waiting to be realized. This is her time—right now, right here. The Indigenous woman who has carried generations on her back, who has walked through fire and silence, who has dreamed while broken and built while hurting—she stands tall in her fullness.

No longer a footstool beneath the weight of others, she rises as a throne, sovereign and unshakable. The voices of her ancestors echo in her heart, reminding her that justice is already flowing in her favor. The world shifts as she claims her space unapologetically, radiating divine light without needing glitter or noise to prove it.

Her story is no longer whispered in shadows but sung from mountaintops. She is the oracle, the prophet, the healer, and the queen. She is the embodiment of resilience, power, and sacredness. The veils have lifted, the masks have fallen, and her true essence shines brighter than ever before.

Her time is now.

And so it is.

Chapter 25: She Who Chooses Herself

In reality, peace of mind is not always easy to find—not after all you've been through. Trauma has a way of lying to you. It whispers that you are alone, that there's no backup, no support, no love, no hope, no redemption. But trauma couldn't be more wrong.

You have more backup than you can count. And most of it? It's supernatural. It's invisible but undeniable. Divine. Ancestral. Celestial. Sacred. There are forces working in your favor even when you sleep. Powers greater than the systems that tried to break you.

They tried to make you forget how to live, especially when they bring the bitter past and smear it onto your present. But let this chapter be your interruption. You will be just fine. You are not meant to carry everything. Don't buy into the illusion. Don't allow pain to be recycled in your mind. Don't get carried away by what was. Because what will be—is greater.

Yes, trauma changes how you think, how you trust, how you dream. It attempts to shrink your capacity and cast shadows over your confidence. And somehow, through all of it, you still function. You still rise. You still give. You still build. You even try to absorb the pain of others to spare them—because you know too well how it feels to be hurt. And yet, some of those very people turn around and hurt you again. But the lesson is this: the same way you had to learn and transform through your pain, so must they. It's not your role to save people who choose to harm you. You are not a footstool. You are not a sponge for other people's trauma. You are not a dumping ground for broken souls unwilling to grow. That is not your burden to carry.

Your future is bigger than that. So look up. Look beyond. Look within. Use the frustration as fuel. Transmute the pain into power. Remember what works, who's guided you this far, what you survived. Link yourself to the Higher Power within you—the One who kept you steady, who fed you when systems poisoned the land, who protected you when you didn't know you needed it.

The truth is, they want you frustrated, distracted, and defeated. That's how systems stay in control—by breaking your self-image. They don't want you to see your own brilliance, your genius. But the veil is thinner now. You are closer to your breakthrough, your dreams, your destiny than you even know.

If you're reading this, you're already rising. You're doing the work. You're getting free. And you're doing it unapologetically.

You are not defeated unless you consent to be. You've taken a stand for everyone else—now it's time to take a stand for yourself. Be loyal to your healing. Be devoted to your own peace. No more being everyone else's emotional shield. You are not the anti-shock absorber of the world.

Live your life. Fiercely. Gently. Boldly. Boundaried. Spiritually. Divinely.

Declare. Invoke. Protect. Revere. Affirm. Rebuild.
And this time, start with you.

Affirmations: I Choose Me

- I choose myself unapologetically.
- I am no longer the dumping ground for other people's pain.
- I carry the wisdom, not the weight.
- I protect my energy and honor my essence.
- I am supported by divine and supernatural forces.
- I live from the power within me, not the fear around me.
- I forgive wisely, not wastefully.
- My life belongs to me now.

Invocation: Calling on the Power Within

Power within me,

Rise like the sun after a long, dark night.

Lift me above the memories that try to drown me.

Anchor me in the peace I deserve.

Reveal to me the strength of my own spirit. Show me the face of the Divine that lives inside of me.

I call back my energy. I call back my clarity.

I call back my joy. And I refuse to carry what does not belong to me.

Declaration: I Am No Longer Their Shield

I declare:

I will no longer be the protector of those who injure me.

I declare: I am no one's emotional sacrifice.

I declare: I release the trauma and retain the wisdom.

I declare: My peace is sacred and off-limits.

I declare: I will live fully, loudly, boldly, with no shame.

I declare: I am guided, protected, empowered by a Force greater than me.

Prayer: For Peace After the Storm

Holy Spirit,

Divine Ancestors,

Force of Life,

Thank you for bringing me this far.

Thank you for every breath

I still take despite the heartbreak.

I surrender my fears and make space for peace.

Show me how to protect myself without becoming hard.
Teach me to love myself as much as I have loved others.
Surround me with clarity,
with angels, with ancestors, with wisdom.
Help me live this life not in fear, but in fullness.

Amen. Ashe. Ase. Adjye. So be it.

Conclusion

You made it to the end, but in truth, this is only the beginning. May every page you've read rewire your spirit and realign you with your sacred self. May every prayer, affirmation, and declaration break the chains that were never yours to carry.

You are not broken—you are becoming. And this world has yet to witness the fullness of your power. So go forth, beloved, with boundaries, with vision, with divinity. Build. Heal. Maintain. Rise. Shine.

Because this time—you choose you.

Notes.

Plans.

Aha Moment